# The Wonder of Christmas

# ACTIVITY BOOK

## MELODY CARLSON

ILLUSTRATIONS BY JILL WOOD

CROSSWAY BOOKS · WHEATON, ILLINOIS
A DIVISION OF GOOD NEWS PUBLISHERS

*The Wonder of Christmas Activity Book*

Copyright © 1999 by Melody Carlson
Illustrations © 1999 by Jill Wood

Published by Crossway Books
A division of Good News Publishers
1300 Crescent Street
Wheaton, Illinois 60187

First printing, 1999

Printed in the United States of America

ISBN 1-58134-130-X

| 15 | 14 | 13 | 12 | 11 | 10 | 09 | 08 | 07 | 06 | 05 | 04 | 03 | 02 | 01 | 00 | 99 |
|----|----|----|----|----|----|----|----|----|----|----|----|----|----|----|----|----|
| 15 | 14 | 13 | 12 | 11 | 10 | 9 | 8 | 7 | 6 | 5 | 4 | 3 | 2 | 1 | | |

# *Introduction*

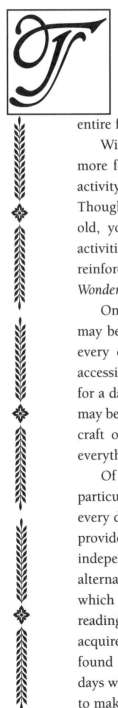

his activity book is a companion to *The Wonder of Christmas* by Melody Carlson and has been developed to help you and your children focus on the true meaning of Christmas. The goal of this book is not to create more things to do during the busy holiday season, but instead to provide activities that will help the entire family remember the importance of Jesus' coming to earth.

Within these pages you will find instructions, ideas, patterns, and more for each day during the month of December. There is a primary activity for every day that is meant to be used with your children. Though these are developmentally appropriate for children 3–10 years old, younger children will need help and/or adult supervision. The activities are intended for you to work on as a family or group and will reinforce what children will be learning from each day's reading in *The Wonder of Christmas*.

On the next page you will find a list of the common materials that may be needed on a regular basis. You will not use each of these items every day, but it would be good to have them on hand and easily accessible when it's time to use them. Any special materials you will need for a day's activity will be listed with the instructions for that day. These may be something you already have on hand or could require a trip to the craft or fabric store. You'll want to look ahead to be sure you have everything ready in advance.

Of course, this is a busy time of year and, depending on your particular situation, it may be impossible to tackle the primary activity every day. Because of this, on many days an alternative activity has been provided. Most of these are fun worksheets that children can do independently. They can be found at the back of this book. These alternative activities are also geared to reinforce the reading for that day which is in *The Wonder of Christmas*. A few of the activities suggest the reading of another children's book. These of course would need to be acquired in advance. The specific alternative activity for each day is found at the end of the instructions for that day's primary activity. On days when no alternative activity has been indicated, you are encouraged to make every effort to complete the primary activity.

To get the most out of this book, sit down with your calendar and decide in advance what activity you will do each day. By planning ahead you can make sure that any special materials are available. Also, try to make this a normal part of your day. By doing so your children will learn in a practical way that the most important thing about Christmas is the celebration of Christ's birth. What a great thing to impress on young hearts!

However you choose to use this book, we hope that each activity will prove a lasting reminder of how God created this special season for a glorious purpose—and that you will creatively and joyfully celebrate *The Wonder of Christmas!*

## *M*aterials you may need:

- ❖ multi-colored construction paper
- ❖ typing paper – 8 $\frac{1}{2}$" x 11"
- ❖ old Christmas cards, Christmas gift-wrap, or rubber stamps
- ❖ cardboard or poster-board
- ❖ white glue
- ❖ felt-pens, crayons, or water-color paints
- ❖ hole-punch
- ❖ scissors
- ❖ baking supplies and ingredients
- ❖ glitter, cotton balls, yarn, ribbon, beads, twine

## December 1 – FAMILY JOURNAL

**Special materials needed:** 2 sheets of 8 ½" x 11" poster-board, 31 sheets of 8 ½" x 11" blank paper, 30" ribbon or yarn

Use 2 sheets of poster-board to create your Christmas Family Journal book-cover. Decorate cover with old cut-up Christmas cards, photos, glitter, lace, etc....

Insert blank sheets of paper between front and back cover. Use hole-punch to punch holes about one inch apart along left side of the journal. Lace yarn or ribbon through cover and pages to "bind" book. Each page will be used to "journal" as the family reads through *The Wonder of Christmas* book and will provide a place to answer the questions at the end of each section. This journal can be saved as a family keepsake to treasure for Christmases to come.

**ALTERNATIVE ACTIVITY:** None

## December 2 – LUMINARY LANTERNS

**Special materials needed:** 1 glass jar for each person, multi-colored tissue paper, votive candles

Cut or tear multi-colored tissue paper into 1" pieces. Mix white glue and water (50/50) in saucer. Dip tissue pieces (one at a time) into glue solution then apply to jar until it is covered, overlapping and smoothing edges of tissues. Using a brush or finger, coat entire surface with glue/water solution. After jar dries, place 1" of sand or kitty-litter in bottom and set small votive candle inside. When lit, the luminaries resemble stained glass and serve as a symbol of God's love shining through us.

**ALTERNATIVE ACTIVITY:** See page 45

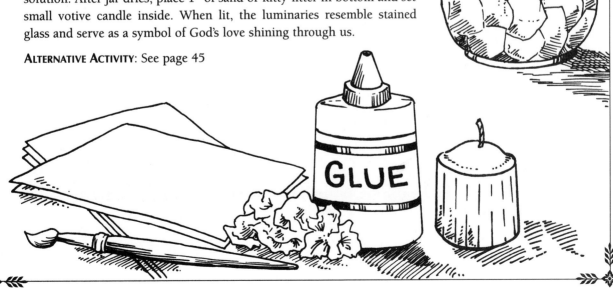

## *December 3* – CHRISTMAS WREATH

**Special materials needed:**   Metal wreath frame (or metal hanger), thin florist wire, red bow, evergreen boughs

If you can, take a walk with your children and collect evergreen boughs like cedar, pine, fir, or holly. Use this time to discuss how evergreens are a symbol of God's everlasting love/eternal life for us. If this is not possible where you live, check with your florist or Christmas tree lot for pieces of evergreen.

Use a wreath frame (circular metal piece available at most craft stores) or simply shape a wire hanger into a circle. Securely attach short pieces of evergreen (one at a time) with florist wire to frame. Be sure to point stems in same direction as you work until entire frame is covered with greens to create full wreath. Place a large red bow over the place where you began. Point out to children that red is symbolic of Christ's blood; green is symbolic of everlasting love/eternal life.

**ALTERNATIVE ACTIVITY:** See page 46

## *December 4* – POPCORN CRANBERRY GARLAND

**Special materials needed:**   White popcorn, fresh cranberries, needle, 6' lengths of thread

Pop white popcorn (be sure to pop plenty so children can eat some). Thread needle and double thread into 3' lengths. Take fresh cranberries (found in produce section of supermarket) and using long, sharp needle, string popcorn and cranberries onto 3' lengths of thread (small children need supervision with this). Tie the individual strands together to create a garland. Works best if 3–5 popcorn pieces are used between each berry. Red berries symbolize Christ's blood; white popcorn symbolizes purity when cleansed by His blood. Use these garlands to decorate Christmas tree.

**ALTERNATIVE ACTIVITY:** See page 47

## *December 5* – RAINBOW ORNAMENTS

**Special materials needed:**   Multi-colored tissue paper

Cut rainbow shape from page 17 and use as template. Trace shape onto poster- or cardboard and cut out shape. Punch hole in marked area and tie with yarn or ribbon (for hanger). Cut or tear 1" pieces of tissue paper (red, orange, yellow, green, blue, violet) and then pinch pieces into small fluffy wads; apply a stripe of glue to outside edge of circle and fill in glue with red tissue; next strip with orange, etc. until all strips are in place. Repeat the same process on reverse side. Let dry and hang on tree. Rainbows are a symbol of promise—God's promise to us is for redemption.

**ALTERNATIVE ACTIVITY:** Simply have children color rainbows with crayons, markers, watercolors, or colored pencils.

## December 6 – HOMEMADE CHRISTMAS CARDS

**Special materials needed:**    Old Christmas cards, wrapping paper, glitter, tissue, stamps, etc.

Use blank construction paper or card stock to fold into cards, then decorate accordingly to be given to friends, neighbors, teachers, family.

**ALTERNATIVE ACTIVITY:** None

## December 7 – LAMB ORNAMENT

**Special materials needed:**    Cotton balls, cardboard, 2 black beads or buttons, yarn

Cut out lamb pattern from activity sheet. Trace pattern onto brown cardboard and cut out shapes. Punch hole on top of back as indicated and thread yarn through for hanger. Use black felt-pen to darken feet and nose. Shred cotton balls and glue onto both sides of body to create fleece. Glue black bead for eye on each side; hang on tree.

**ALTERNATIVE ACTIVITY:** See page 48

## December 8 – CANDY CANE COOKIES

**Candy Cane Cookie Recipe**

Mix together:
  ½ cup shortening
  ¾ cup sugar
  1 tsp. vanilla
  2 egg whites (beaten)

Add:
  1 cup flour
  ½ tsp. salt
  ½ tsp. baking powder

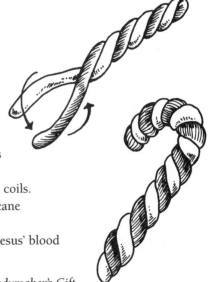

Divide dough into equal halves. Add red food coloring and ½ tsp. peppermint extract to one half and mix until dough becomes dark pink. Wrap dough separately in plastic wrap and chill.

Take walnut-sized ball of each dough color and roll into two 6" coils. Twist two coils together to make "barber pole" and then bend into cane shape. Bake on cookie sheet for about 6–9 minutes at 350 degrees.

Candy cane is symbolic of shepherd's crook; also, red signifies Jesus' blood and white cleansing forgiveness.

**ALTERNATIVE ACTIVITY:** Read *The Legend of the Candy Cane* or *The Candymaker's Gift*

## December 9 – Ten Gifts of Love

**Special materials needed:** Yarn or ribbon

God's gift to the children of Israel was ten rules to live by. Jesus' gift to us is the law of love and grace. On ten pieces of 5 ½" x 8 ½" paper have each person (preschoolers will need help) write out ten special gifts they can give to others this Christmas season but don't have to buy. These can include hugs, smiles, kisses, songs, kitchen-help, dog-walks, back rubs, etc. Then scroll and tie each gift with red yarn or ribbon. Instead of waiting for Christmas, begin dispersing these throughout the holidays. You can use the "To/From" slips found on page 21 as well.

**ALTERNATIVE ACTIVITY:** None

## December 10 – Baking Project

Bake mini loaves of bread to share with friends or neighbors as a reminder of Ruth's generosity to Naomi when she gleaned wheat for their bread.

**Applesauce Nut Bread**

| | |
|---|---|
| 1 cup sugar | 2 cups flour |
| 1 cup applesauce | ½ tsp. salt |
| ¼ cup vegetable oil | 1 tsp. baking powder |
| 2 eggs | 1 tsp. soda |
| 3 Tbsp. milk | ½ tsp. nutmeg |
| | ½ tsp. cinnamon |
| | ½ cup chopped nuts |

Mix sugar and wet ingredients until well blended. Mix dry ingredients separately, then add to wet and blend together. Stir in nuts. Pour batter into greased and floured mini-loaf pans (makes three small loaves or one large loaf). Bake at 350 degrees for 25–30 minutes.

**ALTERNATIVE ACTIVITY:** See page 49

## December 11 – Family Praise Carol

Select a familiar Christmas carol tune and create your own lines and verses to make your special family praise carol. It can be a worshipful song, or just plain fun!

> **Example:** "Jingle Bells" (melody)
> Jesus lives! Jesus lives!
> Jesus lives in me!
> I'm so glad to sing God's praise
> For Jesus lives in me!

Make sure you record your song's lyrics in your Christmas journal. If possible, record your family singing this special song. It will provide enjoyment and laughter for years to come.

**ALTERNATIVE ACTIVITY:** None

## December 12 – GLORY CHAIN

Cut 1" x 4" colored strips of construction paper. On these strips use felt-pens, crayons, or glitter pens to write down all the names you can think of for Jesus/God (i.e. Father, Creator, Savior, Lord, Jehovah, Living Water, Redeemer, Prince of Peace, Lion of Judah, The Rock, King of kings, Messiah...). Use glue to make these strips into links to create a paper chain to hang on tree.

**ALTERNATIVE ACTIVITY:** See page 50

## December 13 – HOMEMADE CALENDARS

**Special materials needed:**    Photocopies of page 19, yarn or ribbon

For each calendar you want to make, photocopy the calendar master page 12 times (page 19). Children can fill in blank pages with month names and day numbers (a good task to keep them occupied when mom's busy wrapping packages). Cut out and glue each calendar grid-sheet onto an 8 ½" x 11" piece of construction paper about ¼" from the bottom. Then decorate upper blank area with art using collage, glitter, drawings, or even photos. Hole-punch at top and lace together with yarn/ribbon and hanger. These make wonderful gifts for grandparents.

**ALTERNATIVE ACTIVITY:** See page 51

## December 14 – CHRISTMAS HEART COOKIES

**Christmas Heart Cookie Recipe**

Mix together:
- ½ cup margarine or butter
- ¾ cup sugar
- 1 tsp. vanilla
- 1 egg (beaten)

Add:
- 1fl cup flour
- ½ tsp. salt
- ½ tsp. baking powder

Chill dough, then roll out on floured board to cut. Use heart-shaped cookie-cutter, then decorate with red and green sprinkles. Bake 7–9 minutes at 350 degrees.

Arrange heart cookies on plate and give to friends or neighbors. Have children color and fill out To/From tags found on page 21 and attach to plates. And don't forget to explain to them that the heart exemplifies how God loved us so much that He gave us Christmas!

**ALTERNATIVE ACTIVITY:** See page 52

# $\mathcal{D}$ecember 15 – ANGEL ORNAMENT

**Special materials needed:** Large piece of white fabric, cotton balls, string/thread, white tissue paper, pipe cleaner, glitter

Cut out 12" circles of white fabric. Place 2–3 cotton balls in center of circle then gather fabric and tie with string as shown (puff creates head). Fluff out remainder of fabric to make "skirt." Accordion-fold white tissue paper (8" sq.) to create wings, and tie with thread as shown. Sew thread hanger through head. Attach pipe-cleaner halo in back. Use white glue sprinkled with gold glitter to adorn edges of wings, skirt, halo. Use black felt pen to make spots for eyes and mouth, and apply a little blush to cheeks. Hang on Christmas tree.

**ALTERNATIVE ACTIVITY:** See page 53

STUFFING FOR HEAD

TIE STRING TO FORM HEAD

FAN OUT

TIE ON WINGS

# $\mathcal{D}$ecember 16 – CELEBRATING BABIES

Take time to pull out old baby pictures (or baby books) of your children and yourself. Enjoy again how special babies are— how unique—how perfectly created by God. Share memories of when your babies were born, how thrilled you were, and what a miracle new life is. Consider how old Elizabeth must have felt after she had all but given up on ever having a baby.

**ALTERNATIVE ACTIVITY:** See page 23

## December 17 – CREATE A FAMILY POEM

This can be serious or simply fun—poetry or prose. It can be a poem of praise or a silly Christmas rhyme, perhaps even in the form of limerick. Invite every member of the family to contribute a line or a verse (depending on ages). It's a good opportunity to teach young children about rhyming words, as well as a fun outlet for creativity. (Hints for poetry: make lists of rhyming words, count beats to lines by clapping, make up your own words.) But remember, your poem doesn't have to rhyme. Mary's was simply a psalm of praise from her heart.

And don't forget to record your poem in your Christmas journal.

**ALTERNATIVE ACTIVITY:** None

deer

sphere hear

here clear ear shear dear mere

## December 18 – MINI CHRISTMAS TREES

**Special materials needed:** Green and yellow construction paper, glitter, yarn, ribbon, sequins, beads, glittery things for ornaments

A Christmas tree is a symbol to remind us of God. Evergreen boughs remind us of God's everlasting love for us. The cone shape of the tree points upward, reminding us to focus our hearts and thoughts upward to God. The star reminds us of the star of Bethlehem, and the lights remind us that Jesus is the Light of the world.

Cut out cone-shape and star patterns from page 25. Trace the cone shape onto green construction paper. Cut out the cone shape, cutting the slits as marked for the star. Glue the edges together to form the Christmas tree cone. Decorate it with sequins, glitter, mini garlands. Trace the star onto yellow construction paper, making a hole-punch in the center for the hanger. Decorate with glitter, sequins, or anything shiny to use as ornaments and garlands. Thread the yarn hanger through the star. Spread some glue on the bottom of the star and slide it into the slits on top of the "tree." Allow to dry thoroughly and hang on your Christmas tree.

**ALTERNATIVE ACTIVITY:** See page 54

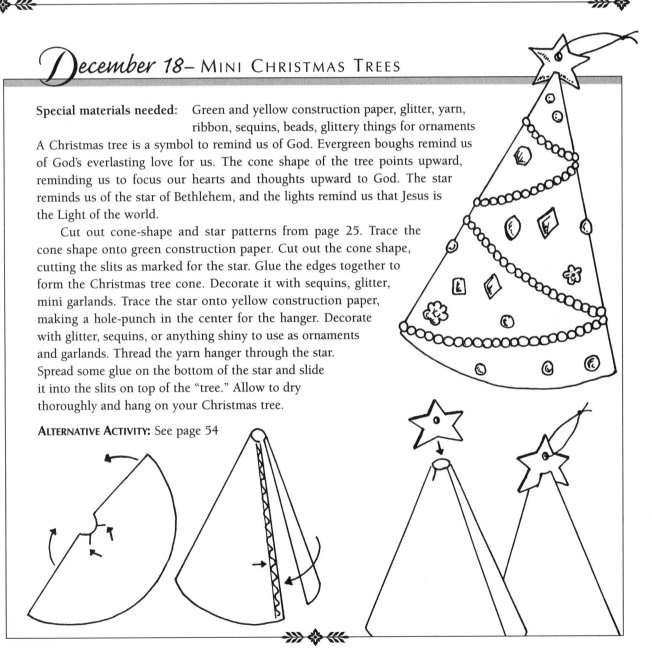

## December 19 – WORLD ORNAMENTS

**Special materials needed:** Small, round balloons, blue tissue paper, brown/green/gold tissue paper, yarn or ribbon

Inflate small round balloons to about 3"–4" diameter. Paper-maché over balloon's surface by using torn strips of blue tissue paper dipped into a mixture of ½ white glue and ½ water. Allow to dry a bit to make handling possible. Draw a rough outline of the continents onto the globe. Use pieces of tissue paper (brown/green/gold) to create the "continents." Allow globe to fully dry until hard (overnight). Deflate balloon. It is not necessary to remove it from inside the globe. Attach the yarn/ribbon hanger to the top. Use "globe" as tree ornament and a reminder that God has the whole world in His hands.

**ALTERNATIVE ACTIVITY:** See page 21

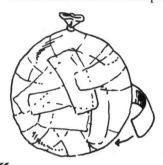

GLUE + WATER

## December 20 – NATIVITY: MARY & JOSEPH

Color the figures (page 27) with felt-pens, crayons, or paint. Mount on cardboard or poster-board and then cut out figures.

**ALTERNATIVE ACTIVITY:** See page 55

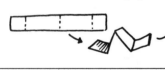

## December 21 – NATIVITY: STAR

**Special materials needed:** Glitter, poster-board, pipe cleaner (optional)

Trace 2 stars onto poster-board using the pattern found on page 29. Decorate with felt-pens, crayons, or paint. Cut out the stars and slide together to form the 3-D figure as shown. Apply glitter along folds and edges. Use the pipe cleaner to attach star above the stable.

**ALTERNATIVE ACTIVITY:** See page 56

## *December 22* – NATIVITY: STABLE

Color the pieces (found on pages 31, 33, and 35) with felt-pens, crayons, or paint. Glue them onto cardboard or poster-board and then cut out the pieces. Construct the stable by inserting tabs into their corresponding slots. Or bend the tabs and tape the pieces together. Add other creative elements as desired: straw/hay, moss, small pieces of wood to make fencing, etc.

**ALTERNATIVE ACTIVITY:** See page 57

## *December 23* – NATIVITY: ANGEL

Color the figure (found on page 29) with felt-pens, crayons, or paint. Mount on cardboard or poster-board and then cut out. Attach the stand to back of figure as shown. Decorate with glitter, sequins, etc.

**ALTERNATIVE ACTIVITY:** Read *The Greatest Gift*, Melody Carlson

## *December 24* – NATIVITY: MANGER & JESUS

Color the figure and manger pieces (found on page 37) with felt-pens, crayons, or paint. Mount on cardboard or poster-board and then cut out. You may want to wrap the baby Jesus with small strips of white cloth. Construct the 3-D manger by inserting tabs into their corresponding slots. Line the manger with small amount of dried grass (hay).

**ALTERNATIVE ACTIVITY:** Read *King of the Stable*, Melody Carlson

## December 25 – LOVE LETTER

Cut out the heart pattern on page 39. Fold white paper in half as shown. Place pattern as shown and then cut out heart-shaped stationery. Decorate the front and use interior to write a personal "love letter" to God.

**ALTERNATIVE ACTIVITY:** See page 58

## December 26 – NATIVITY: SHEPHERD & SHEEP

**Special materials needed:**  Cotton balls, sticks, or pipe cleaners

Color the figures (found on page 41) with felt-pens, crayons, or paint. Mount them on cardboard or poster-board and then cut out. Use shredded cottonballs to create fleece on sheep. Use sticks or pipe cleaners for the shepherd's staff.

**ALTERNATIVE ACTIVITY:** See page 59

## December 27 – NATIVITY: WISE MEN

**Special materials needed:**  Glitter, beads, sequins, etc.

Color the figures (found on page 43) with felt-pens, crayons, or paint. Mount them on cardboard or poster-board and then cut out. Use glitter, sequins, etc. for jewels, crowns, and gifts.

**ALTERNATIVE ACTIVITY:** See page 60

## December 28 – WORD MOBILE

**Special materials needed:**   Two 16" wooden dowels or two wire hangers,
10" to 20" pieces of yarn or string

A visual reminder of all the things that Jesus gives us. Cut out various shapes from construction paper and write on them Jesus' words of life: love, joy, peace, healing, grace, happiness, forgiveness, patience, meekness, etc. Randomly tie pieces of string/yarn to a "cross" of two wooden dowels or sticks. Two wire hangers can also be used. Glue construction paper "words" sandwich-style with cardboard and string in center. Decorate words with glitter, etc. as desired.

**ALTERNATIVE ACTIVITY:** See page 61

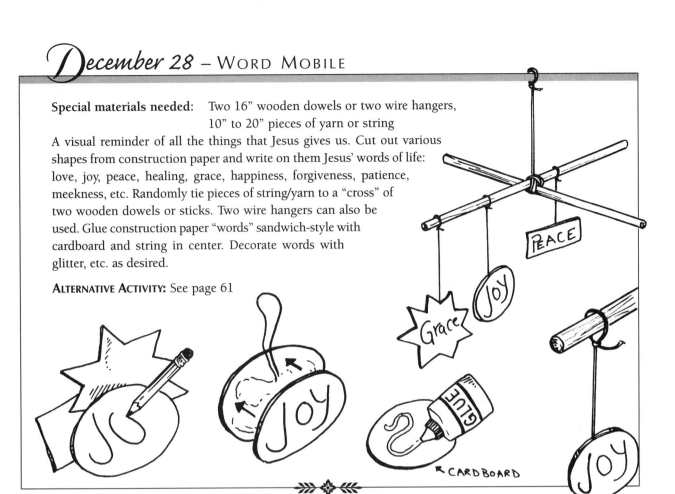

## December 29 – WOODEN CROSS

**Special materials needed:**   Pieces of wooden dowels or sticks,
string/twine/yarn or ribbon, small eye-hook

Using dowels or sticks, break or cut them into 2" and 3" lengths. Bind the pieces together with twine or string to create a cross. Use glue for extra holding. Screw a small eye-hook into the top of the cross. Thread yarn or ribbon through eye-hook to create a necklace or ornament.

**ALTERNATIVE ACTIVITY:** See page 62

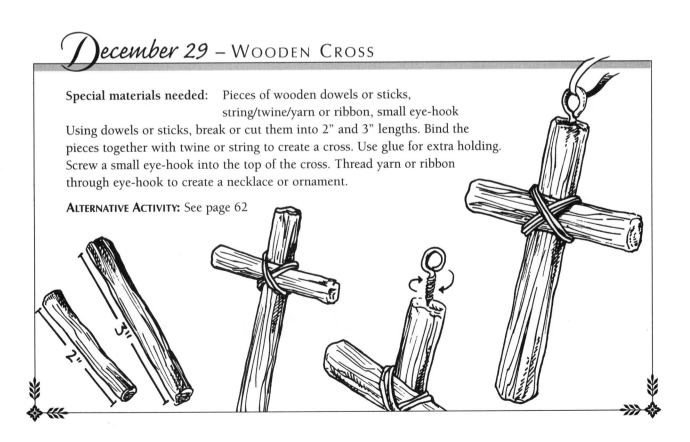

## *December 30* – ORANGE POMANDER

**Special materials needed:** Oranges or tangerines, cloves

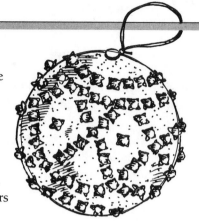

Take small oranges or tangerines and pierce with whole cloves to make pomanders. You may cover the entire orange with cloves, or arrange cloves in patterns. Attach a hanger of ribbon to the top with a pin. This is a reminder of life and death. The orange represents life and the cloves represent preservation and death. (The women wished to use spices to anoint Jesus' body and found it was unnecessary.) Pomanders are preserved by the cloves and will keep for a long time. They can be used ornamentally or as aromatic fresheners for drawers and closets. They also make nice gifts.

**ALTERNATIVE ACTIVITY:** See page 63

## *December 31* – GOLDEN CHAIN

**Special materials needed:** Gold metallic wrapping paper

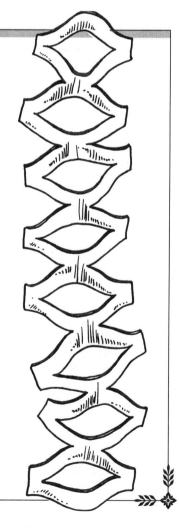

Fold 2 inch-wide strips of metallic gold wrapping paper as shown. Cut as indicated to create Polish chains (see below). Let everyone make several sections and connect them to make one very long chain that can stretch around the house. Young children will enjoy making this chain longer and longer. The chain reminds us of eternity (ongoing chain) and our promise of heaven (gold). You can also use this as a New Year's decoration, then save it to use as a Christmas tree garland in the following year.

**ALTERNATIVE ACTIVITY:** Read *Somewhere Heaven*, Larry Libby

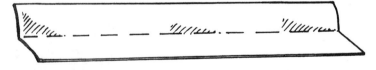

# *Activity for December 5* – RAINBOW ORNAMENT

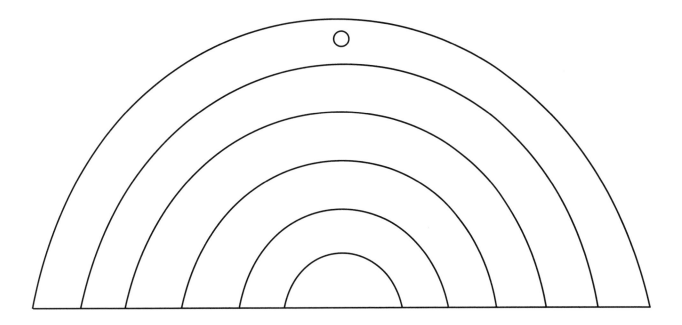

# *Activity for December 7* – LAMB ORNAMENT

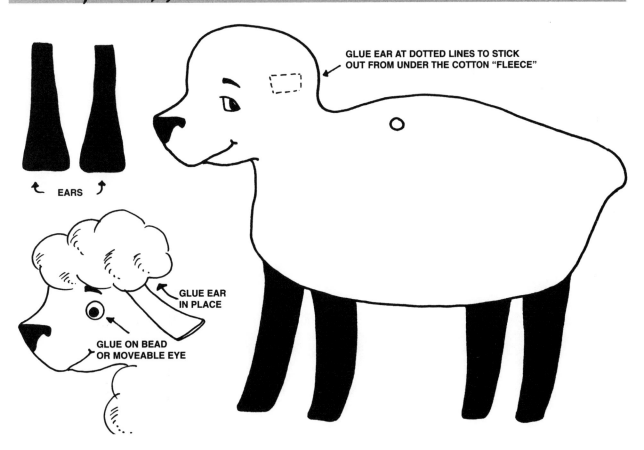

EARS

GLUE EAR AT DOTTED LINES TO STICK
OUT FROM UNDER THE COTTON "FLEECE"

GLUE EAR
IN PLACE

GLUE ON BEAD
OR MOVEABLE EYE

To:

From:

Lovingly made by

To:

From:

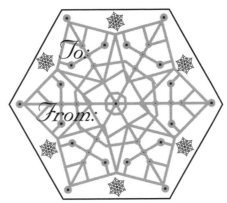

To:

From:

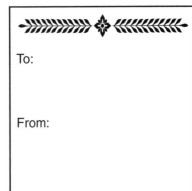

To:

From:

# Alternative activity for December 19

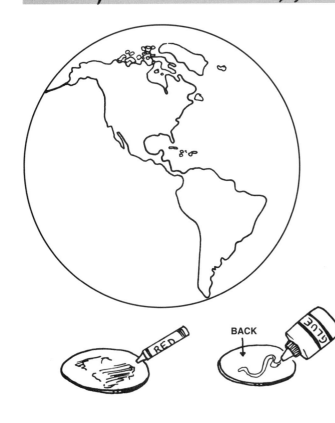

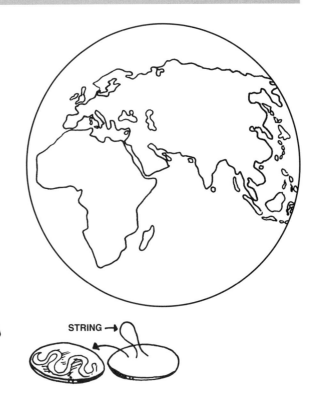

BACK

GLUE

STRING →

RED

*Lovingly made by*

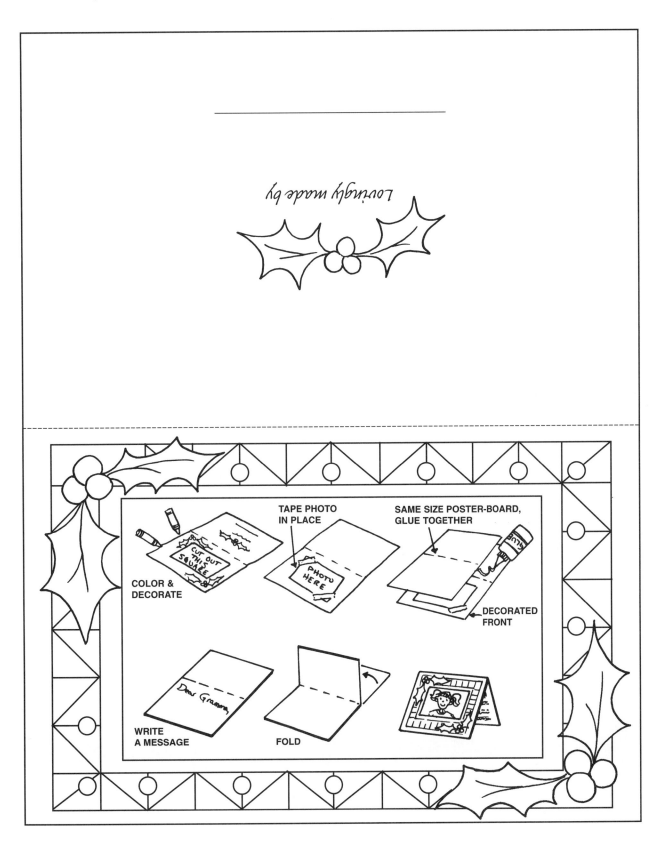

COLOR & DECORATE

TAPE PHOTO
IN PLACE

SAME SIZE POSTER-BOARD,
GLUE TOGETHER

DECORATED
FRONT

WRITE
A MESSAGE

FOLD

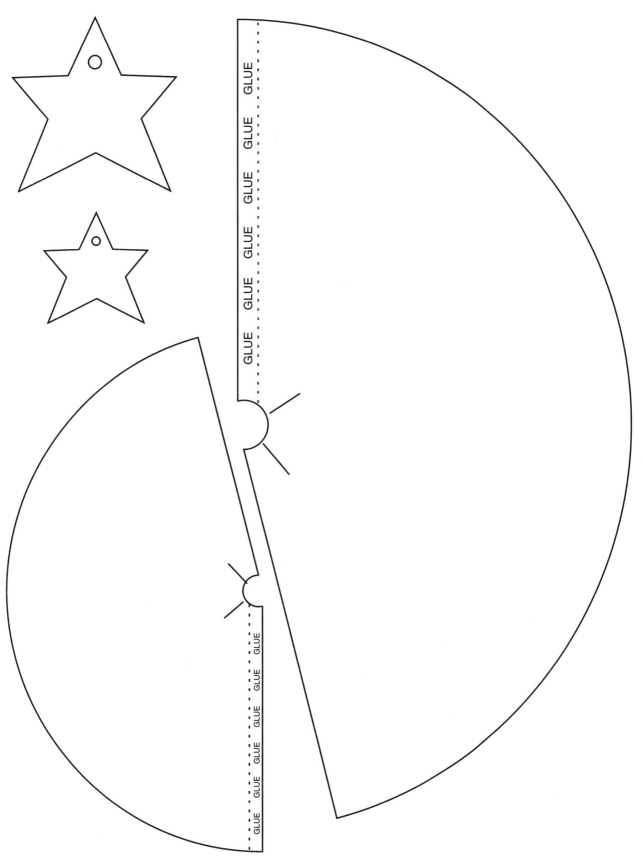

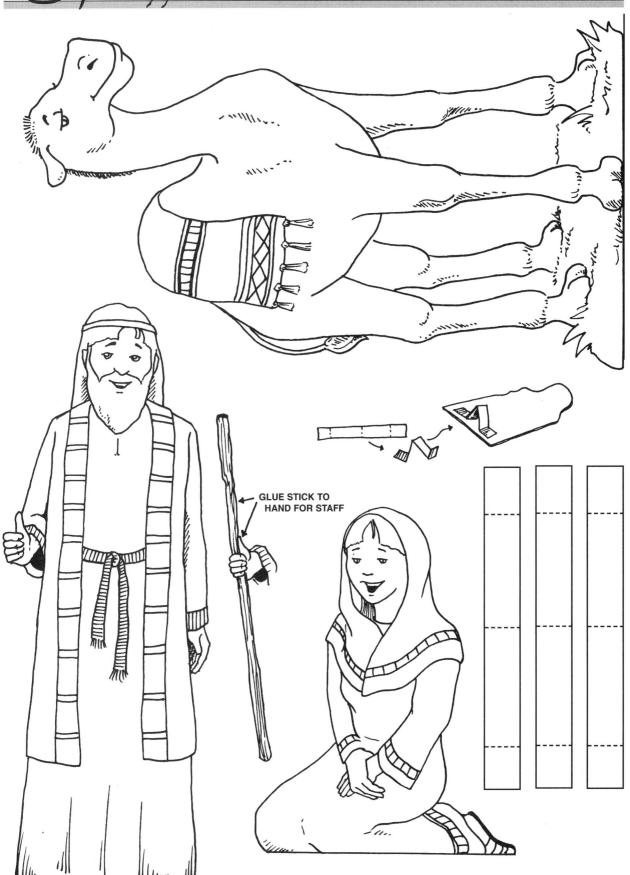

GLUE STICK TO
HAND FOR STAFF

# *Activity for December 21* – NATIVITY: STAR

Cut 2 stars out of poster-board or colored paper. When cutting the slits in the center of the star, cut one to the halfway-mark from the bottom, and one down from the top.

If desired, cut along the internal half star line, careful not to cut through the center.

Color or decorate with markers. Slide stars together as shown below. Fold internal star shapes along fold line to create a more decorative star. Decorate with glitter along the edges and in the creases.

The star can be set on the stable roof, or attached to a pipe cleaner and appear "over" the stable.

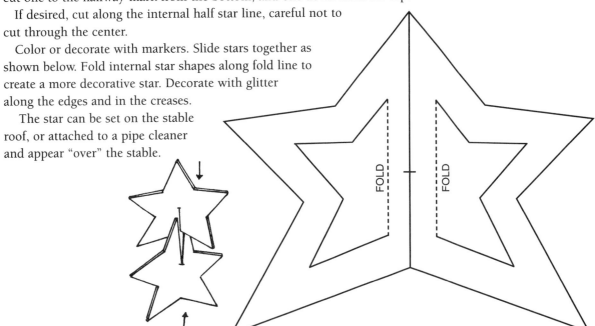

# *Activity for December 23* – NATIVITY: ANGEL

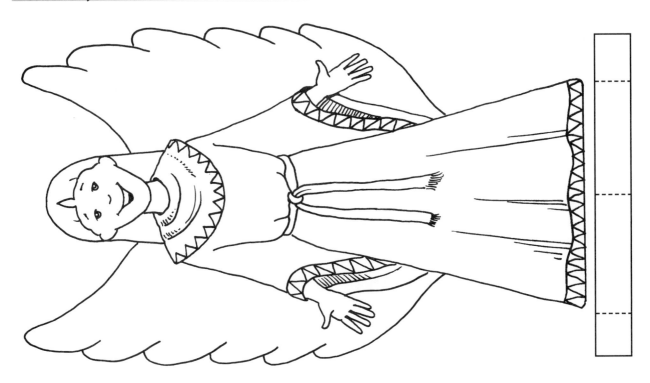

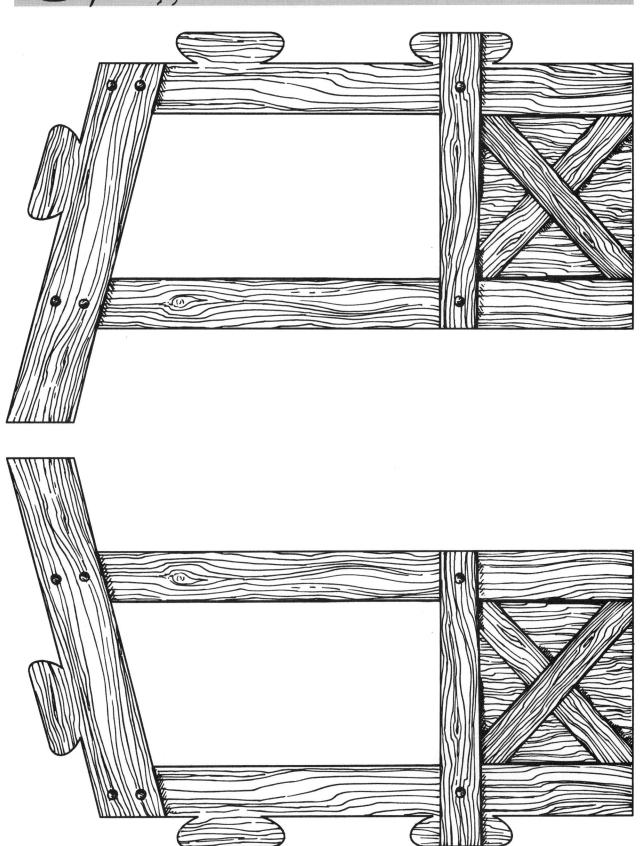

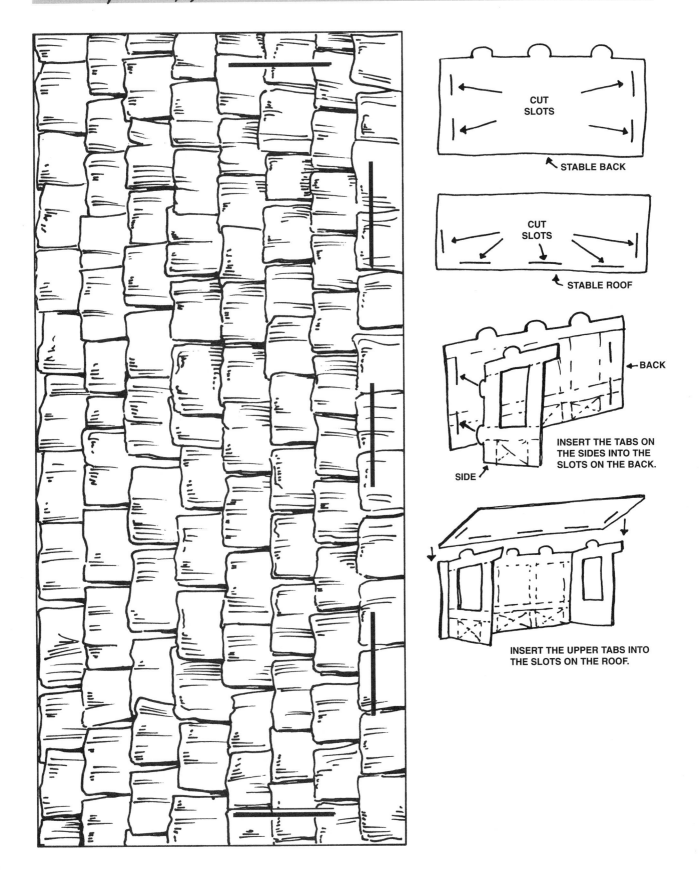

CUT
SLOTS

STABLE BACK

CUT
SLOTS

STABLE ROOF

BACK

INSERT THE TABS ON
THE SIDES INTO THE
SLOTS ON THE BACK.

SIDE

INSERT THE UPPER TABS INTO
THE SLOTS ON THE ROOF.

**VARIATION**: Use two pieces of paper, the outer one a color (red) and the inner one white.

Fold the papers together and trace the heart pattern on the outer front. Cut both layers of paper at the same time. Staple the papers together along the fold line.

Decorate the front and write your letter on the inner paper.

BEND PIPE
CLEANER TO
FORM HOOK

GLUE TO
HAND

GLUE STICK
TO HAND
AS A STAFF

GLUE OR TAPE STANDS
TO LAMB AND SHEPHERD

CUT OUT LEGS IN A GROUP AND
ATTACH STAND TO BACK

OR

CUT OUT LEGS AND SPLAY THE
FEET TO MAKE THE LAMB STAND

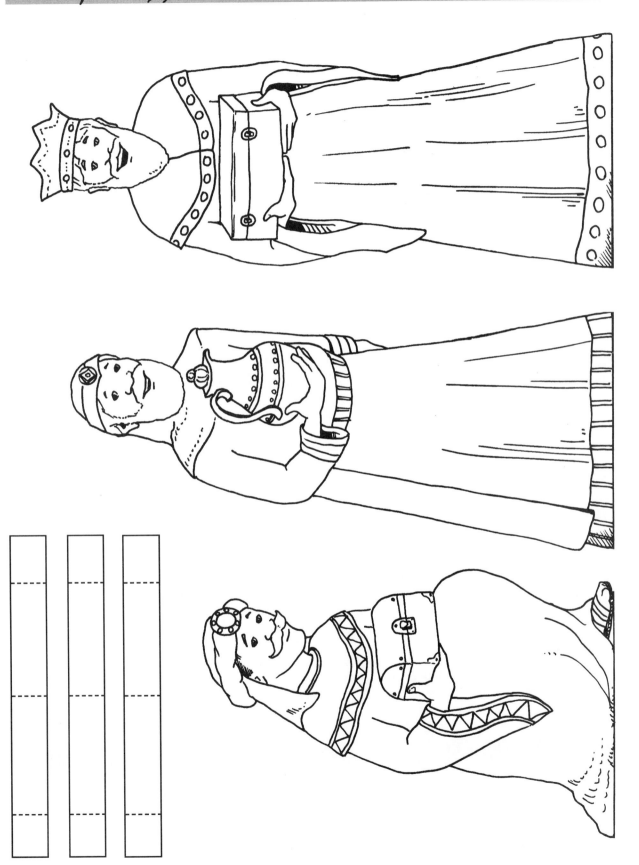

Color this page using the following color key and find a reminder of the light you read about today.

1 = yellow    3 = light blue    5 = white    7 = green    9 = brown

2 = orange    4 = dark blue    6 = red    8 = purple

# Alternative activity for December 3

Can you unscramble the names of these trees?

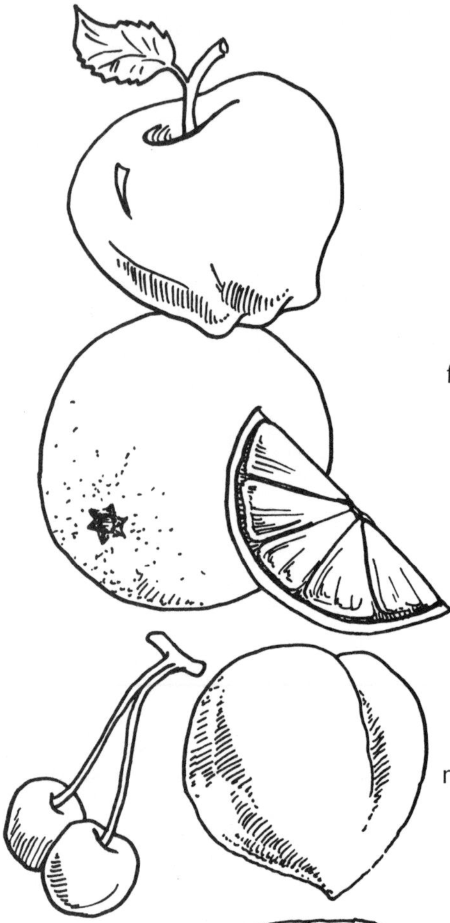

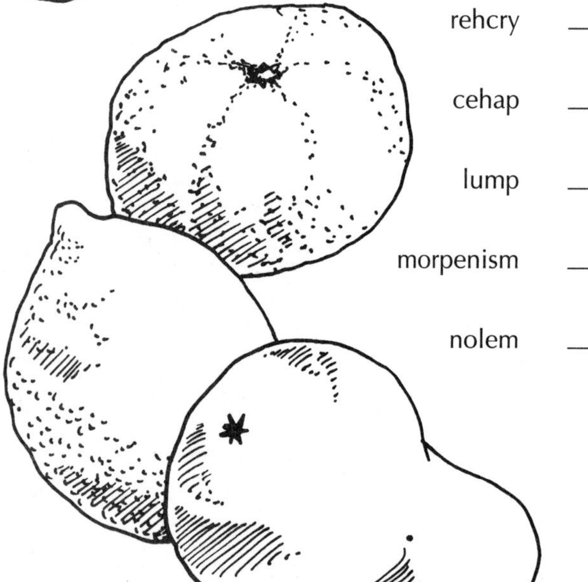

peapl ______________________

gif ______________________

nabaan ______________________

greano ______________________

farguertip ______________________

lovie ______________________

repa ______________________

mile ______________________

lodman ______________________

nigeiranet ______________________

tuccoon ______________________

rehcry ______________________

cehap ______________________

lump ______________________

morpenism ______________________

nolem ______________________

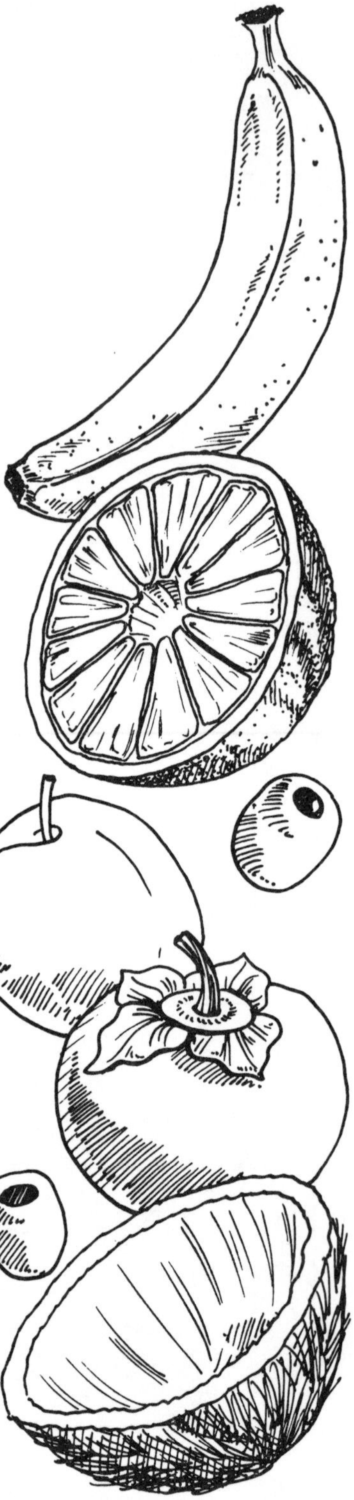

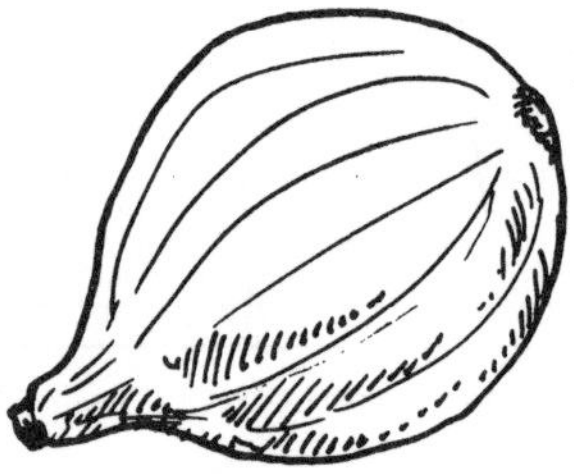

Answers on page 64.

Adam and Eve hid after they disobeyed God. Can you find the following list of hidden objects as you color this picture?

| snake | butterfly | sock | boot | teddy bear | bow tie |
|-------|-----------|------|------|------------|---------|
| fish | arrow | flower | yo-yo | rabbit | moon |

See if you can solve this crossword puzzle about Moses.

ACROSS

1. Who did God choose to lead Israel from Egypt? Exodus 3:10–12

4. Who ruled Egypt? Exodus 3:10–12

6. What sea did the Lord lead Israel to? Exodus 13:17–21

8. What did Israel walk on when crossing the sea? Exodus 14:15–25

9. What 10 things did God send each time Pharoah said "no" to Moses? Exodus 7:14–11:10

11. What did Israel mark with lambs' blood? Exodus 12

DOWN

2. What was Moses before he became Israel's leader? Exodus 3:1–2

3. At night, what was the pillar made of that led Israel? Exodus 13:21–22

5. Which plague hopped? Exodus 8:1–7

7. At what time did the Lord strike the firstborn? Exodus 12:29–30

10. What did God tell Moses to lift at the Red Sea? Exodus 14:15–20

Answers on page 64.

Remember the story of Ruth?  Which pictures would fit into her story?
Color only those pictures.

Answers on page 64.

Prophets in the Bible foretold Jesus' coming. There are a total of 17 books of prophecy in the Old Testament. Can you find the names of these books in the word search below?

| AMOS | ISAIAH | MICAH |
|------|--------|-------|
| DANIEL | JEREMIAH | NAHUM |
| EZEKIEL | JOEL | OBADIAH |
| HABAKKUK | JONAH | ZECHARIAH |
| HAGGAI | LAMENTATIONS | ZEPHANIAH |
| HOSEA | MALACHI | |

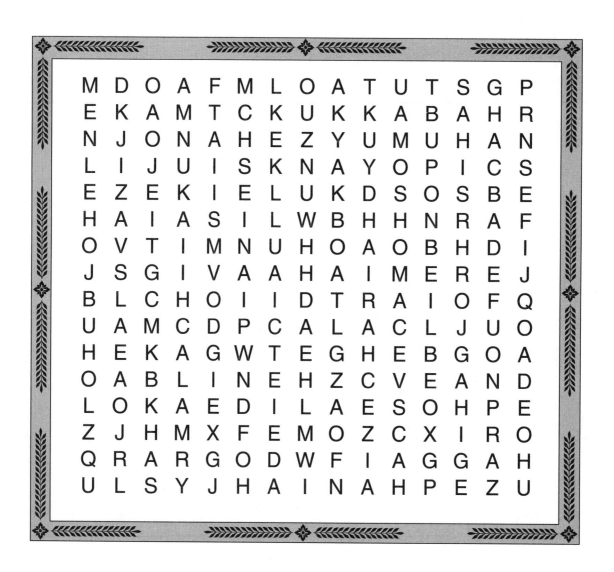

Like putting together a gigantic puzzle, God had many, many things to put in place before all was ready for the birth of His son. Color this picture to get a peek at the first Christmas.

1 = yellow     3 = brown     5 = dark blue     7 = orange

2 = light blue     4 = green     6 = red     8 = light brown

God does and gives many things to show us His love. Can you unscramble these words to see how many ways He loves us?

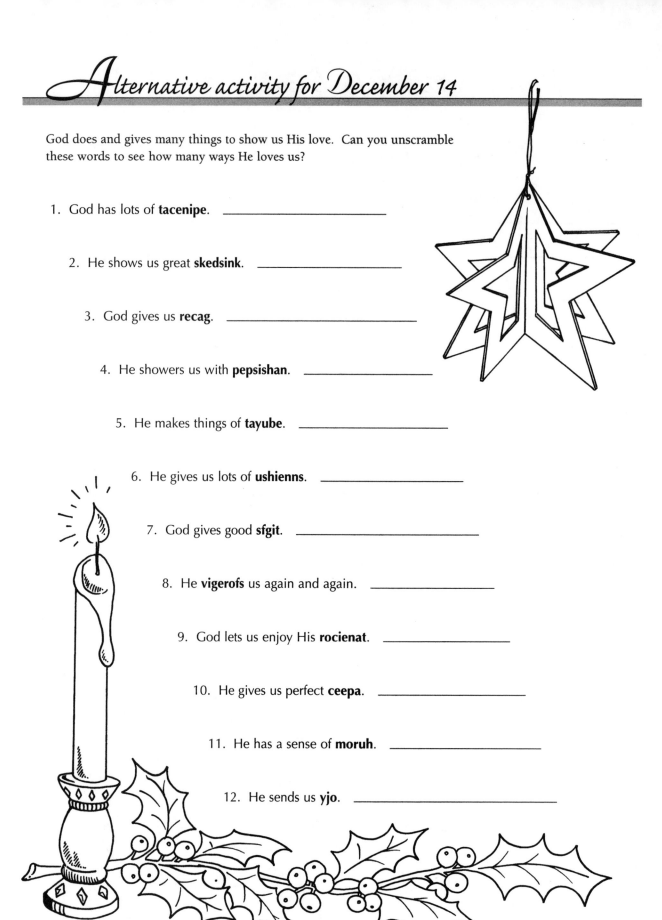

1. God has lots of **tacenipe**. _____

2. He shows us great **skedsink**. _____

3. God gives us **recag**. _____

4. He showers us with **pepsishan**. _____

5. He makes things of **tayube**. _____

6. He gives us lots of **ushienns**. _____

7. God gives good **sfgit**. _____

8. He **vigerofs** us again and again. _____

9. God lets us enjoy His **rocienat**. _____

10. He gives us perfect **ceepa**. _____

11. He has a sense of **moruh**. _____

12. He sends us **yjo**. _____

Answers on page 64.

Every angel here has a matching partner, except for one. Find the pairs of angels as you color them. The one who is different is the angel who came to speak to Mary. Write the name of this special angel under the correct picture. (Clue: the name has 7 letters and starts with *G*.)

Answers on page 64.

An angel came to Joseph in a dream and told him about the baby Mary was soon to have. In the following story (Matthew 1:18-24) some of the important words have been scrambled. Can you unscramble them and use them to complete the crossword puzzle?

This is how Jesus Christ was born. A young woman named **AMYR** (6A) was engaged to **PEHJSO** (1A) from the family of King **VIADD** (3D). But before they were married, she learned she was going to have a baby by God's **YOHL TRISIP** (2D). Joseph was a good man and did not want to embarrass Mary in front of everyone. So he decided to quietly call off the **GENDIWD** (4D).

While Joseph was thinking of this, an **LAGEN** (9D) from the Lord came to him in a **ARMED** (8D). The angel said, "Joseph, the baby that Mary will have is from the Holy Spirit. go ahead and **RYMAR** (6D) her. Then after her baby is born name him **SEJUS** (1D), because he will save his people from their **NISS** (7A)."

So the Lord's **RIMPOSE** (10A) came true, just as the **HOTPREP** (5A) had said, "A **GRINVI** (11A) will have a baby boy, and he will be called **MENAMULI** (12A)," which means "God is with us."

After Joseph woke up, he did just what the Lord's angel told him to do.

## ACROSS

1. _ _ _ _ _ _
5. _ _ _ _ _ _
6. _ _ _ _
7. _ _ _ _
10. _ _ _ _ _ _ _
11. _ _ _ _ _ _
12. _ _ _ _ _ _ _ _

## DOWN

1. _ _ _ _ _
2. _ _ _ _ _ _ _ _ _ _
3. _ _ _ _ _
4. _ _ _ _ _ _ _
6. _ _ _ _ _
8. _ _ _ _ _
9. _ _ _ _ _

Answers on page 64.

Mary and Joseph rode into Bethlehem with the help of a kindly animal. Connect the dots to find its picture. Solve the math problems in order. Plot the dots and connect them as you go along. The first few have been done for you.

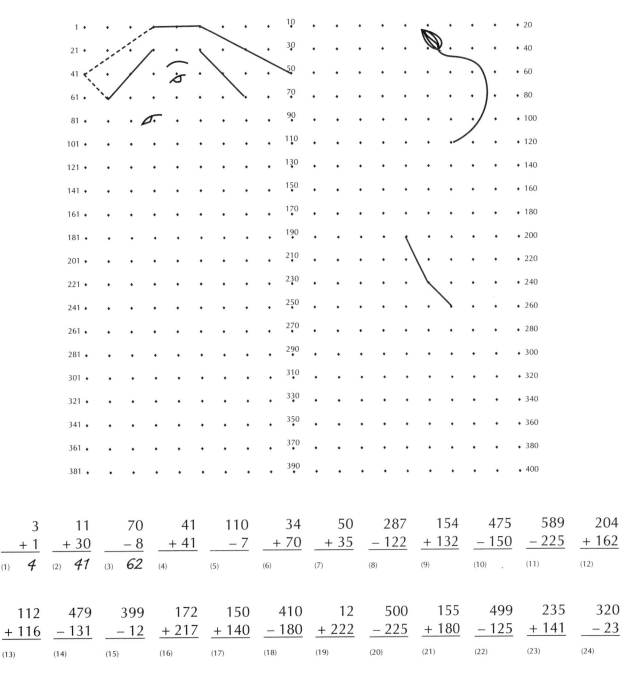

|  | | | | | | | | | | | |
|---|---|---|---|---|---|---|---|---|---|---|---|
| 3 | 11 | 70 | 41 | 110 | 34 | 50 | 287 | 154 | 475 | 589 | 204 |
| + 1 | + 30 | − 8 | + 41 | − 7 | + 70 | + 35 | − 122 | + 132 | − 150 | − 225 | + 162 |
| (1) **4** | (2) **41** | (3) **62** | (4) | (5) | (6) | (7) | (8) | (9) | (10) | (11) | (12) |

| | | | | | | | | | | | |
|---|---|---|---|---|---|---|---|---|---|---|---|
| 112 | 479 | 399 | 172 | 150 | 410 | 12 | 500 | 155 | 499 | 235 | 320 |
| + 116 | − 131 | − 12 | + 217 | + 140 | − 180 | + 222 | − 225 | + 180 | − 125 | + 141 | − 23 |
| (13) | (14) | (15) | (16) | (17) | (18) | (19) | (20) | (21) | (22) | (23) | (24) |

| | | | | | | | | | | | |
|---|---|---|---|---|---|---|---|---|---|---|---|
| 134 | 489 | 173 | 515 | 159 | 145 | 369 | 269 | 95 | 57 | 246 | 27 |
| + 123 | − 211 | + 185 | − 118 | + 240 | + 135 | − 150 | − 110 | + 22 | + 53 | − 178 | + 23 |
| (25) | (26) | (27) | (28) | (29) | (30) | (31) | (32) | (33) | (34) | (35) | (36) |

The wise men are following the star. Connect the dots to see what they are bringing.

Help Mary and Joseph find their way to the stable where Jesus will be born.

This Christmas word find includes 24 words that you have been learning about. They can be found across, down, and diagonally either frontwards or backwards. See if you can find them all.

| ANGELS | KING | PROMISE |
|--------|------|---------|
| BABY | LAMB | PROPHETS |
| CHRISTMAS | LIFE | REDEEMER |
| CROSS | LIGHT | SAVIOR |
| GIFT | MANGER | SHEPHERD |
| JESUS | MARY | STABLE |
| JOSEPH | MESSIAH | STAR |
| JOY | PRAISE | WISE MEN |

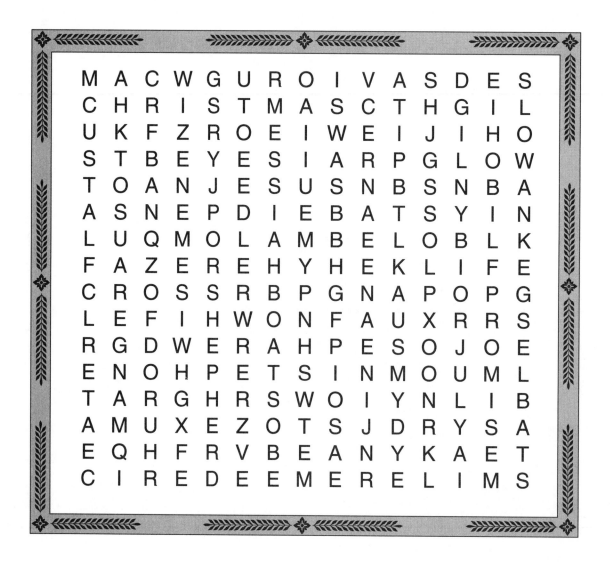

```
M A C W G U R O I V A S D E S
C H R I S T M A S C T H G I L
U K F Z R O E I W E I J I H O
S T B E Y E S I A R P G L O W
T O A N J E S U S N B S N B A
A S N E P D I E B A T S Y I N
L U Q M O L A M B E L O B L K
F A Z E R E H Y H E K L I F E
C R O S S R B P G N A P O P G
L E F I H W O N F A U X R R S
R G D W E R A H P E S O J O E
E N O H P E T S I N M O U M L
T A R G H R S W O I Y N L I B
A M U X E Z O T S J D R Y S A
E Q H F R V B E A N Y K A E T
C I R E D E E M E R E L I M S
```

How many sheep can you find in this picture?

Answers on page 64.

Figure out the secret code to discover what the wise men brought to Baby Jesus. Solve the math problems and then find the letters and write them on top of the lines to spell out the words.

CODE:

| A | B | C | D | E | F | G | H | I | J | K | L | M |
|---|---|---|---|---|---|---|---|---|---|---|---|---|
| 1 | 2 | 3 | 4 | 5 | 6 | 7 | 8 | 9 | 10 | 11 | 12 | 13 |

| N | O | P | Q | R | S | T | U | V | W | X | Y | Z |
|---|---|---|---|---|---|---|---|---|---|---|---|---|
| 14 | 15 | 16 | 17 | 18 | 19 | 20 | 21 | 22 | 23 | 24 | 25 | 26 |

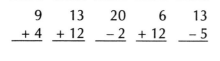

| ___ | ___ | ___ | ___ | ___ | ___ | ___ | ___ | ___ | ___ | ___ | ___ |
|---|---|---|---|---|---|---|---|---|---|---|---|
| 4 | 22 | 9 | 7 | 5 | 12 | 20 | 2 | 8 | 4 | 21 | 3 |
| +2 | −4 | −8 | +7 | +6 | −3 | −6 | +1 | −3 | +10 | −2 | +2 |

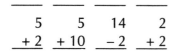

| ___ | ___ | ___ | ___ | ___ |
|---|---|---|---|---|
| 9 | 13 | 20 | 6 | 13 |
| +4 | +12 | −2 | +12 | −5 |

| ___ | ___ | ___ | ___ |
|---|---|---|---|
| 5 | 5 | 14 | 2 |
| +2 | +10 | −2 | +2 |

Answers on page 64.

Jesus said and did many things, but the sentences below are not complete. Can you fill in the missing words and discover some of those things?

1. "I am the Good __ __ __ __ __ __ __ __."  John 10:11

2. Jesus made the __ __ __ __ __ to see.  John 9:19–25

3. "God loved the world so much He gave his only __ __ __ . . ."  John 3:16

4. Jesus __ __ __ __ __ __ on the water.  John 6:19

5. "I am the __ __ __ , the __ __ __ __ __ , and the __ __ __ __ ,..."  John 14:6

6. Jesus __ __ __ __ __ __ the sick.  Matthew 14:14

7. " __ __ __ __ one another, as I have __ __ __ __ __ you."  John 15:12

8. Jesus __ __ __ the hungry crowd.  Mark 8:1–9

9. "Come __ __ __ __ __ __ me."  Luke 5:27

10. "I am the __ __ __ __ __ of the __ __ __ __ __ ."  John 12:46

11. Jesus calmed the __ __ __ __ __ sea.  Matthew 8:23–27

12. "I am the __ __ __ __ __ of life."  John 6:48

13. Jesus made the __ __ __ __ to walk.  Matthew 21:14

14. "I come to bring you __ __ __ __ __ __ water."  John 4:10

15. "Love your __ __ __ __ __ __ __ __ as yourself."  Mark 12:31

16. Jesus performed many __ __ __ __ __ __ __ __ .  Mark 6:2

17. "Do not __ __ __ __ __ others or you will be judged."  Luke 3:37

18. Jesus taught by telling __ __ __ __ __ __ __ __ .  Luke 15:3

19. "I go to prepare a __ __ __ __ __ for you."  John 14:3

20. "I am with you __ __ __ __ __ __ ."  Matthew 28:20

Answers on page 64.

Who did Jesus die for? Use the secret code to solve the puzzle and find out.

CODE:

| A | B | C | D | E | F | G | H | I | J | K | L | M |
|---|---|---|---|---|---|---|---|---|---|---|---|---|
| 1 | 2 | 3 | 4 | 5 | 6 | 7 | 8 | 9 | 10 | 11 | 12 | 13 |

| N | O | P | Q | R | S | T | U | V | W | X | Y | Z |
|---|---|---|---|---|---|---|---|---|---|---|---|---|
| 14 | 15 | 16 | 17 | 18 | 19 | 20 | 21 | 22 | 23 | 24 | 25 | 26 |

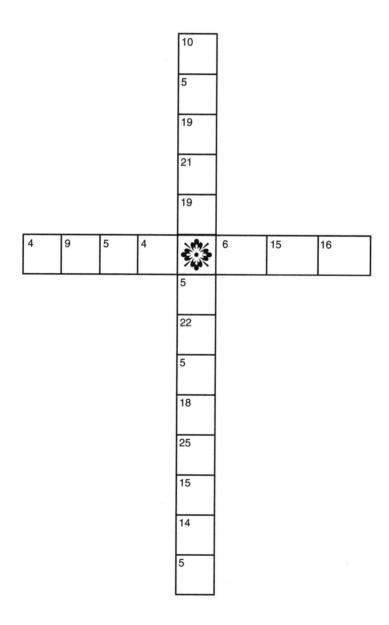

Answers on page 64.

Do you remember what happened after Jesus was killed upon the cross? Can you number these pictures so they tell the story?

Answers on page 64.

December 3:     apple, fig, banana, orange, grapefruit, olive, pear, lime, almond, tangerine, coconut, cherry, peach, plum, persimmon, lemon

December 7:     Across: 1. Moses, 4. Pharoah, 6. Red Sea, 8. dry land, 9. plagues, 11. doorposts
Down: 2. shepherd, 3. fire, 5. frogs, 7. midnight, 10. staff

December 10:    blanket, bread, camel, cart, sandals, sickle, wheat

December 14:    1. patience, 2. kindness, 3. grace, 4. happiness, 5. beauty, 6. sunshine, 7. gifts, 8. forgives, 9. creation, 10. peace, 11. humor, 12. joy

December 15:    The middle angel is different, and this angel's name is Gabriel.

December 18:    Across: 1. Joseph, 5. prophet, 6. Mary, 7. sins, 10. promise, 11. virgin, 12. Immanuel
Down: 1. Jesus, 2. Holy Spirit, 3. David, 4. wedding, 6. marry, 8. dream, 9. angel

December 26:    There are 16 sheep hidden in the picture.

December 27:    GOLD, MYRRH, FRANKINCENSE

December 28:    1. shepherd, 2. blind, 3. son, 4. walked, 5. way, truth, life, 6. healed, 7. love, loved, 8. fed, 9. follow, 10. light, world, 11. stormy, 12. bread, 13. lame, 14. living, 15. neighbor, 16. miracles, 17. judge, 18. parables, 19. place, 20. always

December 29:    solution: Jesus died for everyone

December 30     Top row: 6, 3, 1,
Middle row: 7, 5
Bottom row: 8, 2, 4